THIS BOOK IS FOR

..SIMON . JAMES . BENNETT........
THE WORLD'S MOST ~~STUPID/SEXY/~~
LOVABLE/~~UGLY~~/GOR...
CUTE/ADORABLE/E...

WITH ALL MY LOVE
~~YOURS IN DISGUST~~ . Mum .and .Dad
How could a son of ours be anything else?
P.S. PLEASE TAKE NOTE OF PAGE(S)

You are expected to read this book from
cover to cover and then write a 26,000 word
essay on it to be handed in to your
tutor not later than Feb; 1st 1984

THE AQUARIUS BOOK

A CORGI BOOK 0 552 12314 5

First publication in Great Britain
PRINTING HISTORY
Corgi edition published 1983

Copyright © Ian Heath 1983

Corgi Books are published by Transworld Publishers Ltd.,
Century House, 61-63 Uxbridge Road, Ealing, London W5 5SA

Made and printed in Great Britain by the
Guernsey Press Co. Ltd., Guernsey, Channel Islands.

THE AQUARIUS BOOK

BY
IAN HEATH

AQUARIUS

JANUARY 20 – FEBRUARY 18

ELEVENTH SIGN OF THE ZODIAC
SYMBOL: THE WATERBEARER
RULING PLANET: URANUS
COLOURS: EMERALD, ROYAL BLUE
GEMS: GREEN OPAL, EMERALD
NUMBER: FOUR
DAY: SATURDAY *Because you can die in!*
METAL: URANIUM
FLOWER: GENTIAN

The AQUARIAN at work..............

.... IS PUNCTUAL ....

.... CO-OPERATIVE ....

.... APT TO DRIFT..............

.... FORGETFUL ....

.... WORKS IN FITS ....

..........AND STARTS..............

...... IS EASILY TRAINED........

......HAS FLASHES OF BRILLIANCE..

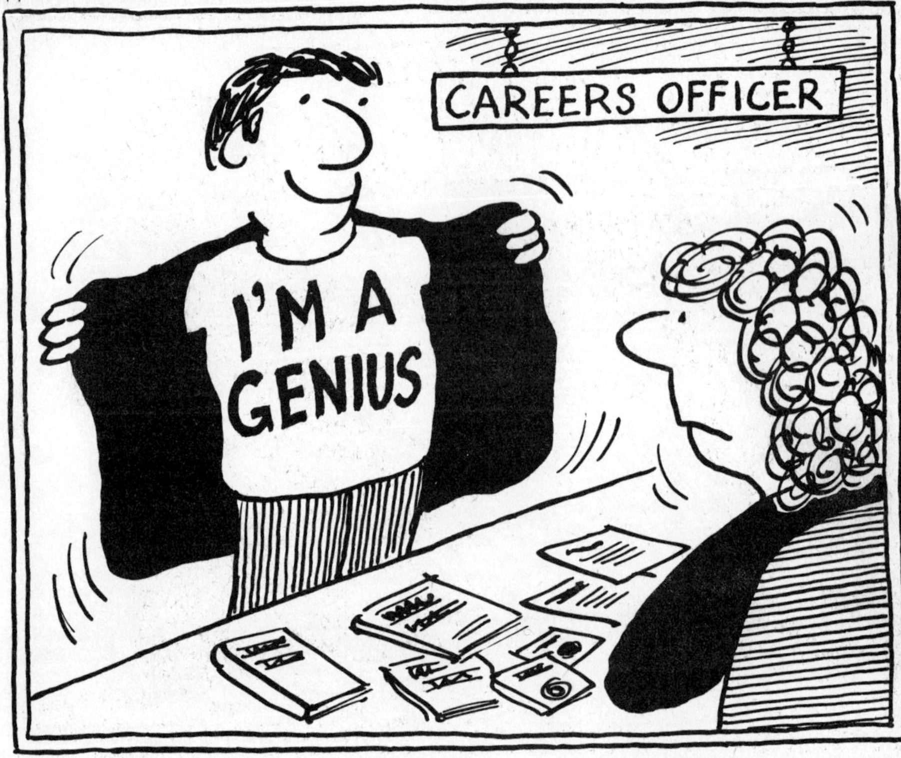

....SHOWS SIGNS OF GENIUS........

...... AND LOVES MONEY. That's true!

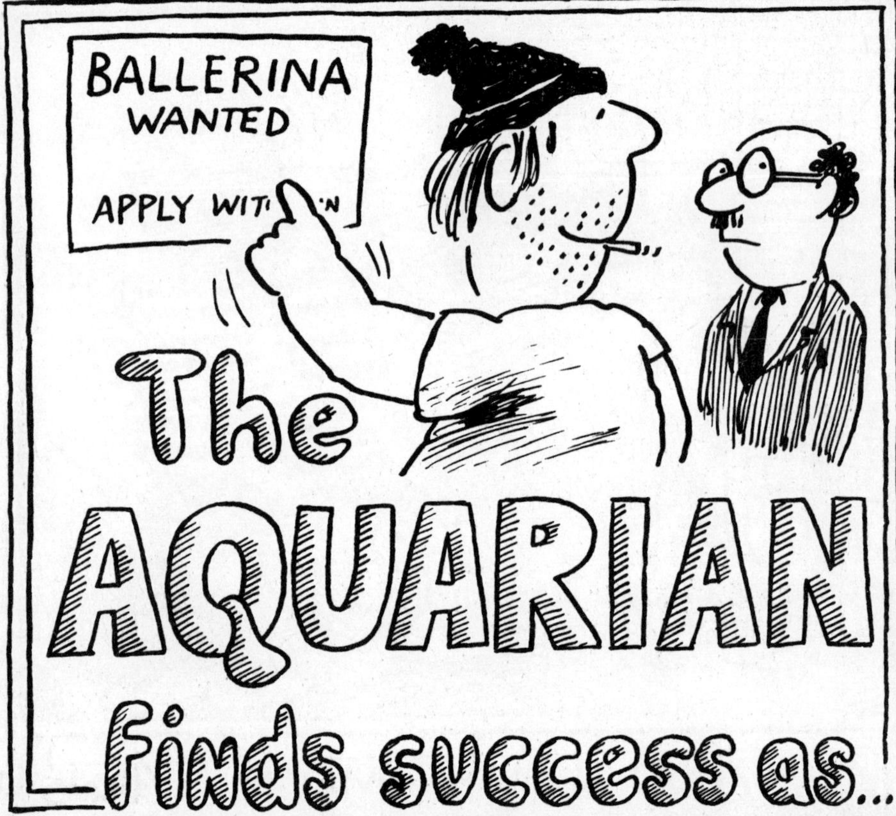
BALLERINA
WANTED
APPLY
The AQUARIAN finds success as....

.... A PILOT ....

.... TEACHER ....

.... FROZEN PEA PACKER..........

.... INVENTOR ....

..........ACTOR..............

.... POLITICIAN ....

.... OR ASTRONAUT.

The AQUARIAN at home...........

.... LIKES LABOUR-SAVING GADGETS..

.... GOLDFISH ....

...... OCCASIONAL SECLUSION ....

.... ENJOYS LUXURY ....

.........LOVES TELEVISION..........

.... ENTERTAINING ....

...... IS PEACE-LOVING ....

.... NEEDS PLENTY OF SLEEP........
But no until after midnight

.... ADORES CATS ....
but only if they look like dogs.

………… AND MUSIC.

The AQUARIAN likes......

............HOLIDAYS................

.... CUSTARD. ~~especially~~ Dad's!

.... GAMBLING............

..... BEING UNCONVENTIONAL ...

.........EXPLORING.............

.........AND VALUES FREEDOM.

The AQUARIAN dislikes ……………

..... BEING TIED DOWN ....

.......CAVIAR AND CHIPS...........

.... ROUTINE ....

.... A POSSESSIVE PARTNER ....

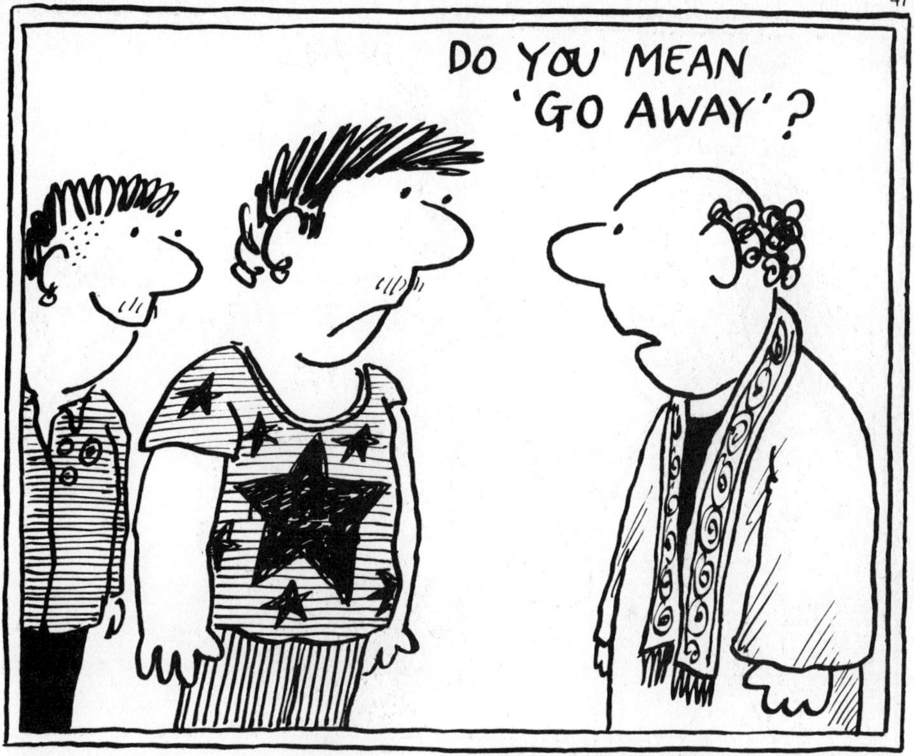

..........BAD LANGUAGE........

........AND PLASTIC FLOWERS.

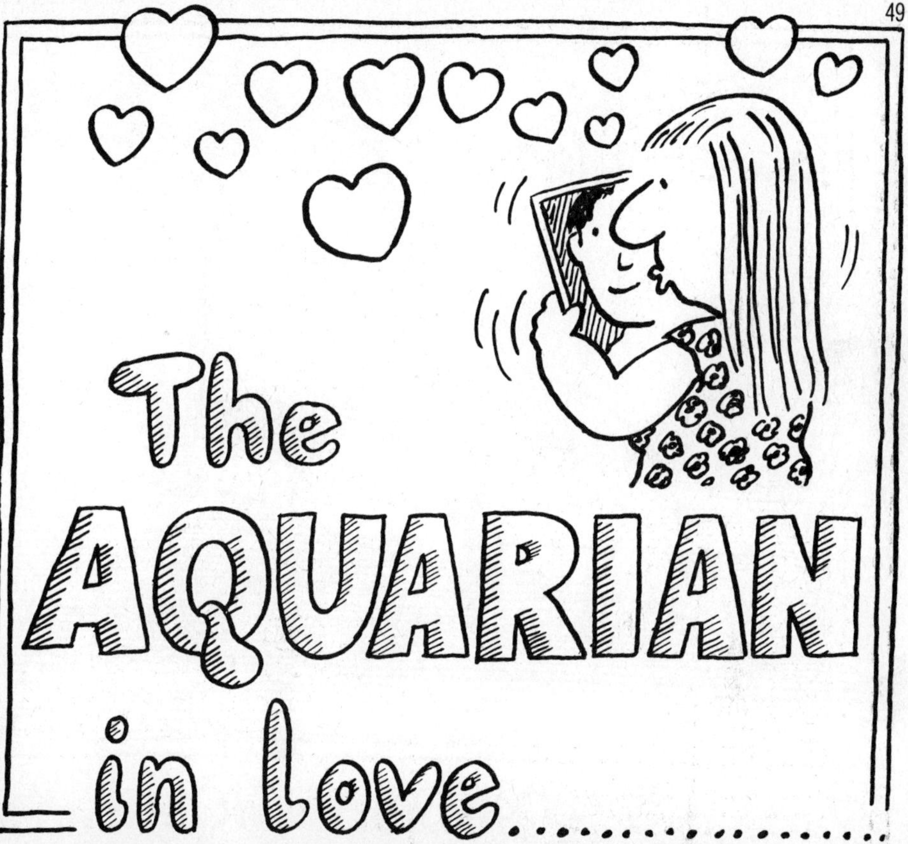
The AQUARIAN in love........

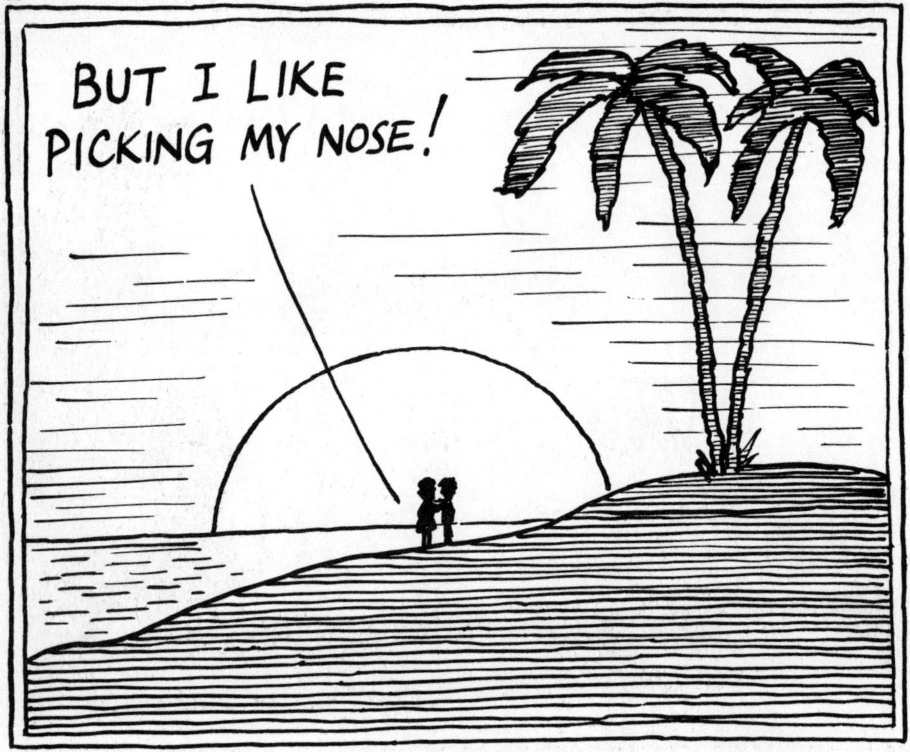

.... IS UNROMANTIC ....

............EXPERIMENTAL............

..... LIKES SEXY CLOTHES..........

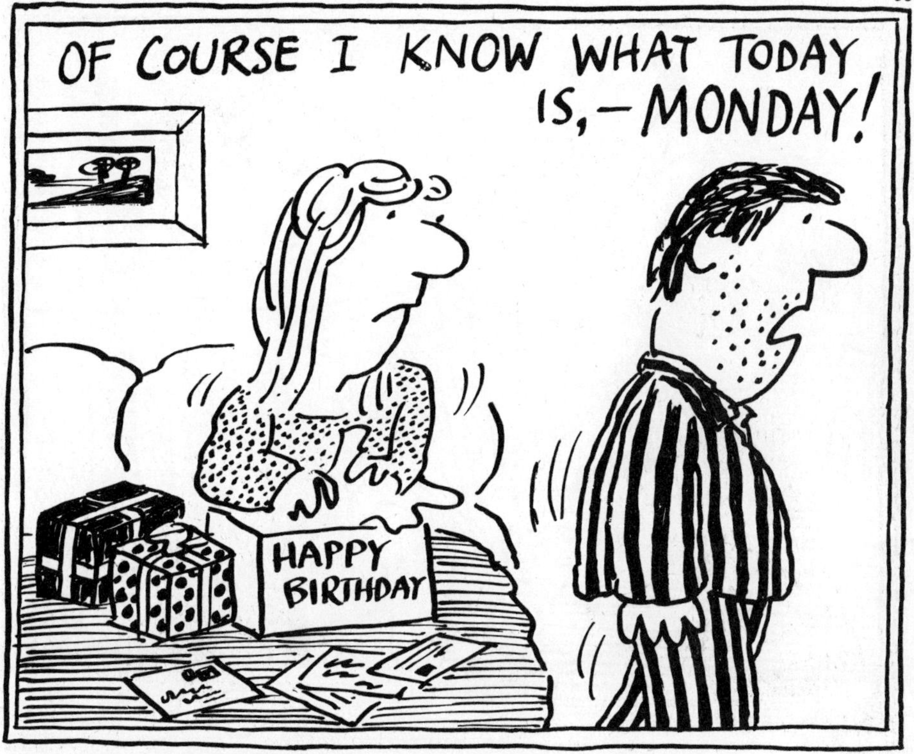

... FORGETS SPECIAL DAYS ....

.... IS SPONTANEOUS ....

.... DETACHED ....

............TRUSTING................

.... COLD ....

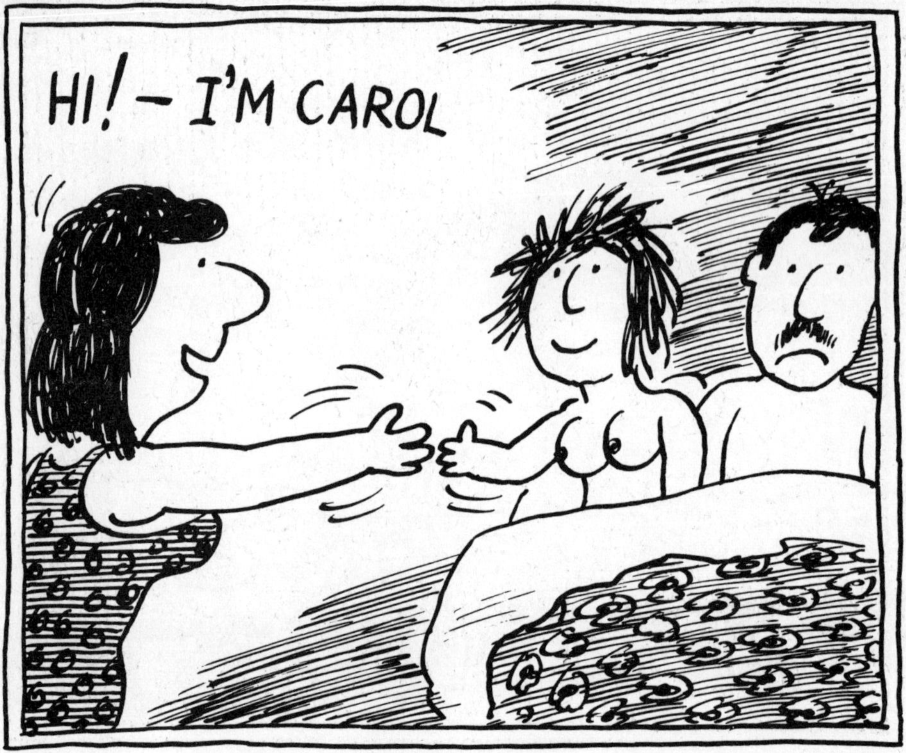

.......NOT JEALOUS....................

.... AND LOVES EVERYBODY.

AQUARIAN AND PARTNER

HEART RATINGS

♥♥♥♥♥ WOWEE !!
♥♥♥♥ GREAT, BUT NOT 'IT'
♥♥♥ O.K. — COULD BE FUN
♥♥ FORGET IT
♥ WALK QUICKLY THE OTHER WAY

♥♥♥♥♥
GEMINI LIBRA
♥♥♥♥
SAGITTARIUS PISCES ARIES CAPRICORN
♥♥♥
TAURUS AQUARIUS
♥♥
LEO SCORPIO
♥
CANCER VIRGO

AQUARIUS PEOPLE

VIRGINIA WOOLF : JULES VERNE
ROBERT BURNS : JOHN BARRYMORE
SHERLOCK HOLMES : CLARK GABLE
HAROLD MACMILLAN : JAMES DEAN
JIMMY DURANTE : LEWIS CARROLL

JACK BENNY : JAMES JOYCE
MARY QUANT : ZSA ZSA GABOR
BARRY HUMPHRIES : YOKO ONO
FARRAH FAWCETT : KIM NOVAK
BURT REYNOLDS : FRANCIS BACON
CAROL CHANNING : ANTON CHEKHOV
CHARLES DARWIN : LEE MARVIN
JACK LEMMON : ABRAHAM LINCOLN
SOMERSET MAUGHAM : MIA FARROW.
W.C. FIELDS : JOANNE WOODWARD
PAUL NEWMAN : RONALD REAGAN

oh dear!